Date June 19, 2012

Dear

To my dear friend
Linda.
Because your special
Happy Birthday

From
Shirley Knab

Because You're Special

© Audrey Jeanne Roberts, licensed by Suzanne Cruise

© 2003 Christian Art Gifts, RSA
    Christian Art Gifts Inc., IL, USA

First edition 2003
Second edition 2012

Designed by Christian Art Gifts

Scripture quotations are taken from the *Holy Bible*, New International Version® NIV®.
Copyright © 1973, 1978, 1984 by International Bible Society.
Used by permission of Zondervan Publishing House. All rights reserved.

ISBN 978-1-77036-747-0

Printed in China

12 13 14 15 16 17 18 19 20 21 – 10 9 8 7 6 5 4 3 2 1

Because You're Special

Audrey Jeanne Roberts

christian art gifts®

Dear Reader

One day, a dear friend I only get to speak with infrequently, called. As we were catching up on our lives, she perceived that I was more than a little weary and frazzled. She stopped in the middle of a sentence, paused and said, "There's something you need to know."

We work in the same industry with many of the same people. To encourage my heart, she shared some of the things people had said to her about me. She told me how much they loved me and about how special I was. Of course it was quite embarrassing, and I was more than a little uncomfortable, but you know it really lifted my spirit!

You may also find it a little hard to read all the wonderful things I want to say to you through this little book. But you need to know how much you're loved, how special people think you are – and more importantly, how special you are to the God who created you!

Audrey Jeanne Roberts

My special friend, I bear in mind
that faithful friends are hard to find.
In you, I've found one good and true
and yearly grows my love for you.

~Audrey Jeanne Roberts

Adapted from Victorian Verse

Contents

Special people — 9

Because you are special — 11

God gave you special gifts — 13

You have a special laugh! — 15

You share my dreams — 18

I believe in you — 20

You keep my confidences — 22

You have wonderful insights — 24

You are such fun to be with — 29

The time we share is twice as special — 33

You are a wonderful listener — 37

God loves you exactly as you are — 39

God has a special purpose for your life — 42

You've helped me grow — 46

Blessed are the merciful,
for they will be shown mercy.

~ Matthew 5:7

Special people

Special people scatter seeds of kindness wherever they go. They are generous and caring, thoughtful and helpful; they are always concerned with the needs of those around them.

Rarely thinking of themselves, they seldom see the beauty their small acts of kindness bring out in others. If ever they looked back, they would see a beautiful field of wildflowers that sprang up as they scattered their seeds of caring along life's way.

You, my friend, are one of these special people whose life has brought beauty to so many.

Thank you!

You're special because
God made you especially to be you!

For we are God's workmanship, created
in Christ Jesus to do good works,
which God prepared in advance for us to do.

~ Ephesians 2:10

Because
you are special

If you are like me, you probably feel quite ordinary. You run through the events of each ordinary day, doing ordinary things in your ordinary manner. But you are not at all ordinary – you are special.

You are the unique and individual artwork of the Master Artist – the Creator of heaven and earth. He carefully fashioned you for His great pleasure. Different from all who have gone before you or will follow after you – He loves every little detail about you!

You're special because
there's no one else in the world just like you.

He who began a good work in you will carry it
on to completion until the day of Christ Jesus.

~ Philippians 1:6

God gave you special gifts

Did you know that before the foundations of the earth were laid God planned good deeds for you to accomplish? He knew the tasks He would prepare for you and He has generously built into your unique personality strengths and skills that would be needed to accomplish those tasks.

If you ever feel inadequately prepared to fulfill the role He has asked you to play, simply ask Him for every additional gift that will be required – for God delights to give good gifts to His children.

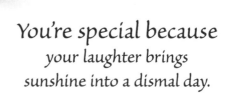

You're special because
*your laughter brings
sunshine into a dismal day.*

You have a special laugh!

You have such a unique and wonderful laugh. I can recognize it in a room full of people and it always makes me smile.

I love that we can laugh and be silly, giggle and play practical jokes. We can see the humor in things no one else can see. Isn't it amazing how our stress can melt away and our joy be renewed by nothing more than a few hours spent laughing together?

God's gift of laughter is priceless – especially when I share it with you.

A happy heart makes
the face cheerful.

~ Proverbs 15:13

You share
my dreams

I feel so safe sharing my hopes and dreams with you. I never worry that you will think I'm foolish. You not only believe in them, but you encourage me to pursue even bigger dreams.

You also remind me of my dreams when I've lost sight of them. You remind me of God's faithfulness, His promises and the things we've prayed for together. You are often God's voice of encouragement to my heart.

You're special because
you're a dreamer of beautiful dreams.

"For I know the plans I have for you," declares
the Lord, "plans to give you hope and a future."

~ Jeremiah 29:11

I believe in you

You are such a special person. I wish you could see yourself as I see you, as others see you, and even more importantly, as God sees you.

I want you to know that I share the dreams you have for your life. I know that God has plans for you that so far surpass anything we can begin to dream of. When they are fulfilled, the joy you feel will be mine as well. I want to be your cheerleader and I can't wait to say, "I knew you could do it!"

You're special because
you don't even know how special you are.

I praise You because I am fearfully and
wonderfully made; Your works are
wonderful, I know that full well.

~ Psalm 139:14

You keep my confidences

It is a special joy to share the deepest things of my heart with you. I trust you implicitly. You have proved yourself a true and faithful friend.

Time spent with you is like being in a safe harbor when seas are stormy. I can express my deepest fears or hurts, my deepest heartfelt emotions and know that you will guard them carefully.

I can always trust you to give me wise counsel with unique and special insights. You let me be real, but also challenge me to greater faith, persistance and endurance.

You're special because

you challenge me to greater faith.

You have
wonderful insights

I love that we often see things so differently. When I think through challenges in my life with you, you always catch important details I might have missed alone.

You see things from a slightly different vantage point that increases my scope of understanding. You help me see options I might have missed or discern God's hand in unexpected circumstances – together we are more than either of us would ever be alone!

You're special because
you look at life with a heavenly view.

"I am God, and there is
no other ... I make known the
end from the beginning."

~ Isaiah 46:9-10

In all my prayers
for all of you,
I always pray with joy.

~ Philippians 1:4

You're special because
you know such great ways to have fun.

You are such fun to be with

You have a way of helping me not take myself quite so seriously. You are such fun to be with – always coming up with fun ways to spend time together.

Some of the most treasured memories I have are of spontaneous, unexpected, and even wacky things we've done together.

We don't do them often enough, do we? Let's plan some fun times to share again soon.

A friendship's value, like the finest art

Your friendship ha.

...creases steadily with the passage of time –
...ecome my treasure.

~ Audrey Jeanne Roberts

You're special because
you grow the sweetest flowers
in the garden of our friendship.

The time we share is twice as special

Time is the most priceless of our riches – and the one we most readily squander away.

Let's not wait until we have "more time" to share, let's work at making more time for each other.

Let's remember to do those ordinary but special things that matter so much – phone calls, a quick note, a spontaneous visit over coffee or tea. We become richer through every moment we spend together.

If we love one another,
God lives in us and His love
is made complete in us.

~ 1 John 4:12

Lord,

Help us to maintain the closeness of our early years through all that life will bring our way. Remind us how important our times of sharing, caring and praying for each other are and show us creative ways to make our time together really count.

We need to be reminded often how precious and important this gift of friendship is. It is like a beautiful garden, help us to tend it faithfully so we can enjoy its bounty for a lifetime.

Amen.

You're special because
you hear the whispers of my heart.

Peace comes to those who linger long in a garden.

You are a
wonderful listener

You listen as much as talk. There's a balanced give and take in our relationship – although most of the time I feel like I'm getting the better end of the bargain!

You're always open to advice as well as able to give wise counsel – you're so sensitive to hold your counsel until I've asked for it.

You hear my heart even when I'm struggling to express things in words. And so many times you read between the lines what I do not even understand myself.

Thank you for listening.

You're special because
God loves you with His whole heart.

God loves you exactly as you are

He accepts you and delights in you, right now, with all your flaws and frailties. There's nothing you could do or be to become more lovely to Him or more loved by Him. You are His special treasure.

But remember that He also loves you too much to let you stay contentedly where you are! He has new adventures for you, new challenges, new things to develop in your character and nature – new ways for you to come to know Him in a deeper and more fulfilling way.

God has poured
out His love into
our hearts.

~ Romans 5:5

God has a special purpose for your life

He has something for you to accomplish that no one else but you can. He alone understands all the twists and turns your life has taken thus far. They don't make sense to you and me now, but one day they will. Not one thing you've experienced in life will have been wasted or is unimportant.

He has walked you through difficult trials, through grievous pain and wearying struggles. He is strengthening you, increasing your abilities and building into you His character so that you can communicate to a lost and lonely world how very much He loves them.

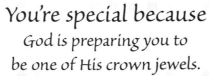

You're special because
*God is preparing you to
be one of His crown jewels.*

Lord,

   Show me ways I can support my friend in finding Your purpose for her life. Show me ways to encourage her, lift her up and be understanding in every way.

   Show me how You see her and the things that You think are really special, help me to be a part of communicating just how much You love her and delight in her.

   Amen.

And let us consider how we may spur one another on toward love and good deeds. Let us not give up meeting together, as some are in the habit of doing, but let us encourage one another – and all the more as you see the Day approaching.

~ Hebrews 10:24-25

You've helped me grow

My life would be so incredibly different today if I didn't have you to share it with. When I feel overwhelmed by the traumas of everyday life, you are there to remind me of my blessings – large and small.

You listen carefully, see clearly and help me put things into proper perspective. God has used you so much to help me grow. I know I am a better person since you became a part of my life.

You're special because
your life is God's love letter to the world.

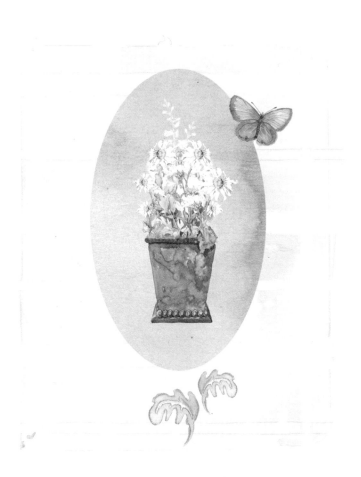